# Contents

# Shapes

There are shapes all around us.

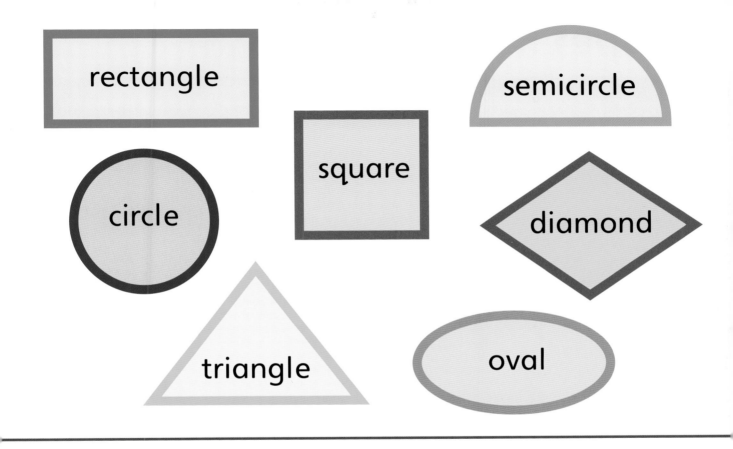

rectangle

semicircle

circle

square

diamond

triangle

oval

Each shape has a name.

# Shapes in gardens

There are many shapes in a garden.

What shape is this shed door?

This shed door is a rectangle.

What shape is this pond?

This pond is an oval.

What shape can you see under this bridge?

The shape under this bridge is
a semicircle.

What shape are these hedges?

These hedges are squares.

What shape can you see in
this flower?

There is a circle in this flower.

What shapes are in this fence?

There are diamonds in this fence.

What shape is this tree?

This tree is a triangle.

There are many shapes in this garden.
What shapes can you see?

# Naming shapes

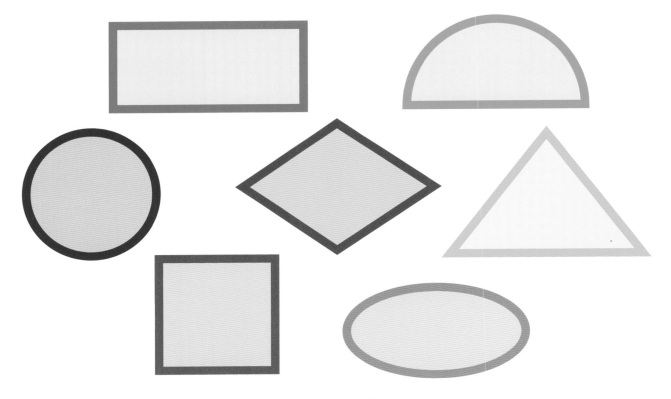

Can you remember the names of these shapes?

# Picture glossary

**hedge** line of bushes, trees, or shrubs planted close together

# Index BETTWS

5-7-18

**Notes for parents and teachers**

**Before reading**

Make two sets of the shapes shown on page 22 out of card. Hold up each shape in turn to the class and ask the children what it is called. Give each child a shape and tell him or her to explore the room looking for things that are the same shape. Explain that shapes can be many different sizes.

**After reading**

Garden collage: cut a variety of shapes from coloured paper (for example, green triangles, brown rectangles and squares, yellow circles, purple diamonds, pink semicircles, and red ovals). Ask the children to use the shapes to make flowers, trees, and bushes. Help them glue their shapes onto paper to make a garden collage.